STORIES, ARTICLES, POEMS & THOUGHTS

By

Azik Chowdhury

Stories, Articles, Poems & Thoughts

This is a collection of stories, articles, poems, and thoughts, I've written over 14 years. I started writing as a way of expressing how I felt.

The first part takes three chapters from each of the books I've published. A Muslim Boy and The Refugee.

I then include articles I have written for two online magazines, Mercurius and The Archer.

And the last sections include poems and thoughts I have written over this time. When travelling I always have a notebook with me, and when something, someone, or a memory makes me think, I try to write. And this section includes those moments.

I DEDICATE THIS STORY TO MY FRIENDS

Stories, Articles, Poems & Thoughts

CHAPTERS

Introduction

I was born in Bangladesh, but in 1972 I moved to London with my family. We were refugees because of the civil war in Bangladesh. While no one knows the actual number of deaths, some people have said, it was as high as three million.

For our first week in London, we stayed in a hotel, and then we moved to Eburne Road, Holloway, London N7. It was a rundown three storey town house. Not too dissimilar to the house, in the television comedy Rising Damp.

1

We were on the second floor, and we had two rooms. The front room doubled up as my Amma and Abba's (Mum and Dad's) bedroom, and the kitchen was the room my sister, Tina and I slept in. A curtain separated the kitchen area and our bed. We shared a bathroom with two other families.

There was an incredibly happy memory of this place. The garden had an Anderson shelter, and for Tina and me, it was our playground. And we were happy, because we understood each other, and nobody stared at us. It wasn't clean, but it was dry. This is a picture of my sister and I, and it was taken in 1970.

Tina is two years older than me, and we were separated when we started to attend Grafton Primary School. It was a strange and scary place, and it was my first experience of racial abuse. I remember being frightened, but since I didn't speak English, I didn't know what those boys were saying. All I remember was the look of hatred.

It took me three months to learn English, and within six months, I was fluent. However, the written language still baffles me, but through reading, research, and writing, I continue to learn.

We then moved to Southeast London when I was ten. A multicultural and vibrant place, but one with many social issues, including racism. On many occasions, I waited at the bus stop on Well Hall Road, where Stephen Lawrence was murdered. A Muslim Boy, my first novel, is set in that environment.

I continue to do a day job, but writing is a passion. Since it gives me the chance to use my imagination.

I truly believe in the words uttered by Beppe in a Muslim Boy. "Always do what you love, when you are doing that, it never feels like hard work."

I have been writing since 2008, and part of the inspiration came from the film Gladiator. In particular the line. "What we do in Life echoes in eternity." Although the film came out in 2000, I didn't see it until 2007, and that's when the itch started. And while these words gave me the initial push, I found that it was an incredibly cathartic process. In writing, I was able to silence some of my demons, and work through irrational thoughts. But it wasn't easy. I had an idea, but not much more. But I guess, you've got to start somewhere.

Since writing my 2nd novel, I have written articles. But I have also included some of my earlier pieces, in the section, Poetry and Thoughts.

A Muslim Boy

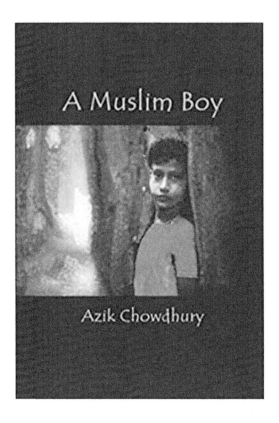

A Muslim Boy was my first novel. It was published on 14th December 2017. It took me a long time to write this. In fact, I started it in 2008.

However, due to my father's death in 2013, I stopped writing for over two years. And when I went back to it, it didn't feel right. And even today, I think it could be better, and I have to stop myself from going back to it. There comes a point, where you have to stop, otherwise, you'll get nothing else done.

People have often asked me. "Is this about you?" And my answer is always the same.

It is what I and others experienced. Some of the experiences were my own, but many weren't. But I express all of these through the eyes of my main character, Shanti Sadan.

Here I include three chapters, Fear, Racism, and Tolerance. Fear is the first chapter, and this is where the story starts. It's September 1976, and it's Shanti's first day at secondary school.

In the chapter Racism, Shanti starts to understand, that most people are kind, and Racists are a minority, although they are the most vocal and violent.

I have also included the chapter Tolerance. When you read Tolerance, it might shock you, but you may be even more shocked, when you learn, that I still carry the scar of the cigarette burn.

These chapters, as well as the entire book, gives balance, to what would otherwise be a very dark story. I try to show, that throughout the hatred there was also love.

I hope you enjoy reading this selection.

A Muslim Boy – Fear

"Come on! Its seven o'clock! It's time to wake up!" As if that isn't enough, three loud knocks thump against Shanti Sadan's bedroom door.

Within a few seconds of this rude awakening, the shrill sound of Shanti's alarm clock rings, and vibrates on the pine bedside table. To him, these noises have ganged up to shatter his sleep. With drowsy eyes, he fumbles for the clock, and manages to turn it off, without knocking it to the floor.

He rubs his eyes, and then he hears the sound of hurried feet running down the stairs. He stares at the clock, and he squints, until it comes into view. It's 7.05 a.m.

His heartbeat speeds up, and it overtakes the rapid second hand of the clock. Pushing his head back against the pillow, he remains motionless. His hands rest on his chest, and he feels the rhythmic and accelerating thumping of his heart. His ears pulse with the sensation, and he thinks he can hear a drumming sound.

He's wide-awake. All traces of tiredness have gone, and a new feeling takes its place. Anxiety. He turns his eyes to the single window, and watches the sunlight penetrate the thin blue curtains. It creates a neon effect, and he blinks until his eyes adjust to the dim light. Turning his head away from the window, he gazes at the 1950's walnut wardrobe. The old couple, who lived in the house before the Sadan's, left it behind.

His new black blazer hangs on the door handle, and it casts an ominous shadow. Even in the faint light, he sees it. It reminds him of a vampire's cape. Propping himself up on his elbows, he gets a better view. The blazer, trousers, shirt, and tie are on a hanger, and his new shoes and bag are on the floor. They're in line with the clothes. His new clothes look stern and unwelcoming. He knows he won't have any fun wearing them.

As he stares at these alien garments, a wave of nausea rises in Shanti's throat, and he turns away as if to vomit. At that precise moment, the noise from a radio distracts him. It comes from his neighbour's house. Although the radio plays every morning. Today, with his senses on red alert, the cheerful sounds irritate him. When his neighbour, Mrs Beulah, opens the back door to let the cat out, the noise becomes louder. Slamming his head back on the bed, he covers his face with a pillow. But the distraction is fortunate, and it replaces the nausea with annoyance.

He hears Mrs Beulah screech out of tune, to a song by Elton John and Kiki Dee, *Don't Go Breaking my Heart*. With his hands over his ears, he slides back under the covers. He wants Mrs Beulah to shut up, but she doesn't.

"Come on Fuzzy, get in girl! There's a good girl." His annoyance turns to anger when Mrs Beulah, rattles the box of cat food. And he thinks. *'What a stupid name for a cat! Fancy calling it Fuzzy!'* Once the cat goes in, the back door slams shut, and the sound fades.

The near silence allows him to remember, the six-week school holidays. He spent his days playing on the common. Sitting next to his friend on the branch of a tree, and giggling. He didn't think about today, but it's here, it has arrived!

His in-built panic button explodes into life. His mouth dries up, and his heart moves into another gear, and he wonders. *'Am I having a heart attack? And if I am, can I stay home?'* He looks down at his chest. He sees the rapid hiccupping movement under his skin. It looks like his heart is trying to escape. Perhaps, his heart wants to hide, just as he does.

It's Monday 6th September 1976. Concorde had her maiden flight. Harold Wilson retired as Britain's Prime Minister. And Viking 1 landed on Mars. To Shanti, none of these events mattered. Since it's his first day at secondary school, and he can think of nothing else. In bed, he remembers a warning from an older boy, going into his second year.

"Don't worry about getting bog washed, it doesn't hurt. They hold yer head down a toilet and flush. You get a bit wet, but it's nothing to cry about."

"Bog washed?" He didn't know such a thing existed. Although the warning was very matter of fact, it filled him with dread. He's thought about this horrible act so often, it now seems inevitable.

The first time he saw his new school, was during a shopping trip, made memorable. When Ma called a rude shop assistant, "haramzada." In Bengali, it means bastard. Although he laughed, the sheer size of his new school, put an end to his joy. He stared skywards, at the imposing four-storey building. It was at least five times bigger than his old school, and it reminded him of Colditz Castle, which he'd seen on television. His imagination soared, and he saw the classrooms being as dark and cold as the cells at Colditz. He saw the boys as prisoners of war, and all of them desperate to escape.

A chink of light illuminates his dark thoughts. And he sees himself as part of the escape team. It gives him a break from his fears, but it doesn't last long. Now, he sees the teachers as the sinister guards, and their evil eyes follow his every move. He pulls on the covers and wraps it around him, in a secure and warm embrace. But the calm, lasts less than a minute. There's another loud knock, and he flinches. Before he can answer, Ma walks in.

"Good morning sleepy. It's the big day! Come on. Get up, get ready and come downstairs. I've made the small chapattis you like. There's fried eggs, and as a special treat, we have gulab jamon!" Ma speaks in a nervous babble, as if she's using Shanti's heartbeat, as the metronome for her words.

Any other day, he'd have leapt out of bed. He loves the sweet, syrupy taste of gulab jamun, with their rich cardamom flavour. But today, fear takes away his appetite. Gazing at Ma's warm brown eyes, he thinks. *'Why can't I stay at home? Ma will never bog wash me.'*

He knows he can't take the day off. To do that, he'd need, at least a broken leg. Or an incurable disease. The night before, Abba, his father, spoke with excitement.

"Shanti your school started in 1892! It's been around since Queen Victoria! Did you know she reigned for over 63 years? I learned this when I was your age. That's amazing!"

Abba's eyes sparkled at the thought, that Shanti's school had such a long history. Shanti didn't share Abba's amazement. The only emotion he felt, was fear.

The family tried to lift his spirits, and even Rani, his older sister, gave advice.

"Don't worry Shanti. It's not scary, and the teachers are very nice. Well, they are at my school. You just have to work hard, and you'll be fine." In part, this was the advice Rani received last year, when she started secondary school. Her second-hand words of wisdom made no sense, and he thought. *'If the teachers are so nice at your school, I should go there.'*

After Ma leaves, Shanti puts on his new uniform, and all the time, his stomach churns a nervous tune. He struggles with his tie, and after tying it in a knot, he

11

gives up, and slips it into his blazer pocket. His blazer is huge. His fingertips barely reach the end of the sleeves, and he remembers moaning the day they bought it.

"Abba, it doesn't fit! It looks like a coat. Abba, it's massive!" Abba didn't budge. And now, Shanti is the unhappy owner of a blazer, which is at least three sizes too big.

Once dressed, he puts his bag over his shoulder and walks to Rani's room. She has a full-length mirror on her wardrobe door.

After flicking on the lights, he walks to the mirror. Under the sixty-watt lightbulb, he stares at his reflection. This is the first time he's seen himself in all his uniform. The out of packet creases, and stiff white-collar dazzles, and holds his neck in an unnaturally upright position. He recognises his face, but nothing else. Staring at his own reflection, he steps closer, and examines the stranger looking back at him. He wonders. '*Is that me? No way? I look like a penguin.*' In confusion, he turns around, just to make sure he's alone. His eyes return to the mirror, but within seconds, he hears Ma shouting. Her voice punctures the silence, and at the same time, shatters his thoughts.

"Baba! Come on! come downstairs! Or you'll be late!" Baba is an affectionate term, but the panic in Ma's voice, makes it sound like an order. With her word still ringing in his ears, he steps onto the landing. His new shoes have smooth leather soles, and they feel treacherous against the burgundy and pink flowery-carpeted stairs. His shoes are going in a different direction to his feet. They appear to have a mind of their own, and just like his heart, they don't want to go to school either.

On entering the front room, Shanti greets Abba with a nervous smile, and Abba returns it with glowing pride.

"Baba, where's your tie?"

He takes it out of his pocket and hands it over. Abba smiles and looks beyond Shanti, to where Ma's standing. Shanti faces her, and when their eyes meet, he notices that her eyes are glistening. Ma feels a mixture of pride and sadness. Ma speeds towards him and gives him a huge hug. After pulling away, she speaks.

"Oh Baba, you look so handsome. Do you have your bag and your pencil case? I've got chocolate biscuits, a packet of crisps, and lemonade. Do you want me to put them in your bag?"

He listens to Ma's tearful words, and nods in response to all her questions. But his head is full of worries, and he can't understand why she's scared. When Ma tries to spoon-feed him, he yells.

"Ma, stop it! I'm not a baby! I'm eleven and a half, and I can feed myself!"

Abba and Ma hear the anxiety in his voice, and they don't punish him. Abba smiles at Ma, and then he looks at Shanti and frowns.

"Enough, leave him alone. He's right. He's a young man now. Baba, come here, and I'll teach you how to do your tie." Shanti stands, while Abba perches on the edge of the armchair. As Abba ties the knot, he explains.

"This is a Windsor knot, and gentlemen wear this on special occasions. Your first day at senior school is a very special occasion. It's your first step to becoming a man. Some people think, the Duke of Windsor invented this knot. Well, if it's good enough for a Duke, it's good enough for my boy! There you are. Perfect." Abba pulls the knot up to the top button and squeezes Shanti's shoulders.

Shanti touches the knot and turns to face Ma. On seeing him, she wipes her eyes with the corner of her sari, and he notices her quivering chin. Now her tears flow freely, and despite wiping them away, her tears are winning the race.

The three of them leave the house together. As they walk, Ma tries holding Shanti's hand, but he pulls away. He wants to be brave, and Ma understands. Abba's taken the morning off work, but the best Ma can do, is see them off.

At the bus stop, Ma talks about her first day at school, and it annoys Shanti. He can't understand why she's saying these things, but he doesn't want to be rude. Instead, he stands closer and leans against her hip. Ma places her hand on his shoulder, and immediately, she stops talking. After ten minutes, the bus arrives, and once on-board, Abba makes Shanti buy his own ticket.

"Okay Baba, now you'll know what to ask for tomorrow. Remember to keep hold of your ticket until you get off the bus."

Shanti spots two unoccupied seats, and he takes the one next to the window. When the bus pulls away, he watches Ma waving. She forces a sad little smile, but all the time she's wiping her eyes. He doesn't take his eyes off her, and he forgets to wave. He's doing his best to hold his nerves together. The last time he felt this uncomfortable, was during a rainstorm. He got soaked, and now he feels the same clammy coldness. Despite being a warm morning, goose bumps rise on his skin.

He sits motionless. He stares out of the window, and again he thinks about bog washing. He wants the bus to break down, or at least, slow down. Now he remembers the Viking 1 spacecraft. He imagines an angry army of Martians visiting Earth. He wants them to whisk him away, as payback for the invasion of their planet. He knows he'll willingly go with them. From what he saw of Martians, in the film, *Invaders from Mars*. They didn't have any genitals, or a bum. To him, that meant. They didn't need toilets, and there'd be nowhere for him to be bog washed.

"Town Centre, next stop!" The bus conductor shouts. He's announced every stop like an over enthusiastic tour guide. With each announcement, Shanti is more agitated, and under his breath, he hisses. '*I wish you'd shut up. You stupid man!*' Two minutes later, there's another announcement, and he knows, they're one stop away. In anger, he glares, as if he's just discovered new psychic powers, which he can use to silence the conductor.

"Come on Baba, it's our stop." Abba tries to sound reassuring, but his tone, gives away his own nervousness. They walk up the High Street in silence, and after passing the shops, they see the sign for Watts Road. Shanti's heart speeds up, and again, he feels sick. He takes a deep breath, and he hopes the feeling will pass.

They follow the seven-foot wall surrounding the school, and Shanti traces his fingers along the bricks. His jaw drops as the towering school gates come into view. To him, it's the open jaws of a carnivorous dinosaur. He gulps, steadies himself, and crosses the threshold.

He now faces the biggest crowd he's ever seen. There's at least two hundred boys, and three hundred parents, and he thinks. *'Why are you all watching me?'* With his eyes on the crowd, he trips. Abba reaches for his hand, and looking into Shanti's eyes, he speaks.

"Look Baba, we're nice and early, it's only 8.45. I promise you'll be fine. And don't worry about your blazer, you'll grow into it."

Abba gives Shanti's shoulder a reassuring squeeze, and Shanti returns it with a half-hearted smile. As for his blazer, he's not sure that he'll ever grow into it. All it did, was make him feel tiny, and even more vulnerable. He stares at the building, and

16

his imagination goes wild. He wonders what monsters lurk inside. He wants Abba to stay with him for the whole day. Plucking up the courage, he looks around, but when a man catches his eye, he jerks his head away. He squeezes Abba's hand, and on feeling the sudden movement, Abba kneels.

"Baba, are you okay?" Shanti steps closer. He puts his arm around Abba's neck. Abba rests his hand on Shanti's waist, brings his mouth closer to his ear, and whispers.

"You look very smart. Just like a young gentleman, and you have your Windsor knot. It will keep you safe." A ghost of a smile crosses Shanti's lips. He carries on looking around, but then he feels Abba squeeze his hand. When he looks up, he sees Abba's jaw tighten. Shanti looks in the same direction, and he sees the cause of Abba's tension.

Thirty feet in front of them, is a rugged unshaven man. The man wears a creased T-shirt, beneath a pair of paint splattered and worn-out dungarees. His steel toe capped boots have a thick layer of mud. He looks like, he's just fallen out of bed and forgotten to wash. One side of his hair sticks up, while the other is flat and greasy, and looks glued to his scalp. The stubble on his face glistens in the sunlight. A cigarette hangs from his lips, and a grey curve of ash balances at a precarious angle. The final insults for Abba, are the tattoos over the man's thick arms. Even from a distance, Shanti sees more tattoos, on his knuckles. No one dares to invade this man's space. Like a ranting lunatic, he manages to isolate himself.

Abba turns his head as if to spit out his disgust. He detests this man, but Shanti doesn't know why.

Looking beyond the tattooed man, Shanti spots a familiar face. It's Billy Wright. Billy was the first boy he fought. It wasn't a real fight. Since neither struck the other. They shouted threats in high-pitched voices, while Shanti attempted the Ali shuffle. This almost ended in disaster. When he stood on his untied shoelace. They swore never to speak to each other. But today, their fear connects them, and they exchange nervous smiles. In those few seconds, they forgive one another. But seeing Billy, reminds him of violence, and another bog washing warning.

"And if you fight, they'll give you a right good kicking. It's just a bit o' water, it don't hurt. Honest."

Attempting to hide his fears, Shanti looks down at his new shoes. As the shiny and unfamiliar brogues stare back at him, he wants his worn and trusted trainers. He knows, if he needs to run away, he won't get far in these shoes. Since the hard unyielding leather hurts the bridge of his feet.

Ten feet away, a boy nestles his head against his mother's stomach. Shanti can see the boy is crying. His mother tries to calm him, but she's embarrassed.

"Don't be silly. Come on, dry your eyes. What will people say? You're in big school now. Come on love! Stop it and be a good boy."

Shanti wants to cry. He knows how frightened the boy is, but he doesn't want to give in to his own fears, and he looks away. He continues to search the crowd. He notices that most of the boys' blazers are too big. Half the boys have their sleeves stitched up, and this forms a thick circular lump by their wrists. A boy standing nearby tries to wriggle free. He scowls when his Mum tries, to straighten his tie and flatten his hair. Shanti hears his Mum screech.

"What's wrong with you? For God's sake, pack it in. You got ants in your pants?" The boy whines.

"Mum, get off, I hate this stuff. Why 'ave I got to wear it?" Shanti agrees, and he thinks. *'He's right. We didn't have school uniforms before. So, why now?'*

Many people struggle to buy these uniforms, and they want to get their money's worth. He overhears two mothers having an annoyed and heartfelt conversation.

"I can't believe how much stuff they need. My husband's done tons of overtime to get this lot, and still, there's more. I'm hoping to get the rest on Saturday." The first mother moans, with a frown so long, it resembles an upside-down horseshoe. Like a double act, they echo each other.

"They must think we're made o' bleeding money!"

One boy stands out. His clothes look tailor-made, and he carries an impressive briefcase, with a combination lock. With a mixture of awe and jealousy, Shanti stares. He's sure the briefcase, is the same as James Bond's in *Goldfinger*.

The noise starts to increase, and people crane their necks. Shanti stands on tiptoes, but he can't see beyond a family standing in front of him. This family is huge, and they block his entire view. They're the fattest people he's ever seen. He's horrified, when he notices, that part of the mother's skirt, is tucked under the elastic of her knickers. Whenever she moves, the skirt rides down, and reveals the top of her buttocks. It looks like two bald men with dimples, trying to escape, and straining for fresh air. Shanti hears her speak to her son.

"Kevin sweetheart, I can see some teachers."

Despite not having seen anything, Shanti tugs at Abba's hand, and Abba smiles. A loud shrill whistle pierces the air, and the woman standing next to him jumps, and it makes him giggle.

The whistle gets everyone's attention, and standing as tall as he can, Shanti sees a smart, but serious looking man, standing at the main entrance of the school building. The man stares at the crowd. The stare is intense, and it unsettles him. He grips Abba's hand, while the man stands motionless, and waits for silence.

"Good morning, ladies, gentlemen, and boys!" He announces in a loud voice. The chattering dies down. Once satisfied, the man carries on.

"Let me take this opportunity to welcome you, to James Watt Secondary School for Boys! My name is

Mr Solomon, and I am the lower school headmaster. Thank you for being here on time today. I would ask parents to leave the premises, and for the boys to follow us into the assembly hall!" His voice booms, and it reaches the furthest corners of the playground.

A hint of a smile flickers across Mr Solomon's lips, but within seconds, it disappears. Again, there's the intense stare. Shanti knows, this teacher is mean and tough, and he views him as. *'The prison commandant.'*

It's now the parents turn to feel scared, and as they leave, they keep looking back with reassuring smiles.

Before leaving, Abba kneels, cups Shanti's hands, and places a neatly folded piece of paper in his palms.

"Baba, I wrote this letter for you. Read it when you get a chance, and we can talk later. Be a good boy, listen to your teachers, but remember, enjoy the day."

Shanti grips the piece of paper as he watches Abba walk away. His gaze alternates between his hands, and Abba's back, until Abba is out of sight. He places the letter in the inside pocket of his blazer. He likes this pocket. It's there to hold secrets.

A Muslim Boy - Racism

"**Lads**, have you seen Miss today. She looks bloody gorgeous!"

Dave shouts, after he spots their drama teacher, Miss Goodyear. Due to the icy conditions, she's wearing a snug roll-neck sweater, but its effect is devastating.

Once the others see her, they stare. Her outfit emphasises her figure, and Shanti thinks. *'Wow! She's stunning.'*

During her lessons, the boys struggle when speaking, or making eye contact. The silence says everything, about the way she captivates them. When the bell rings signalling the end of the lesson, the boys on the front row, force themselves out of their seats. Outside the classroom, Shanti and his friends are eager to talk about Miss Goodyear's curves.

"Bloody hell, did you see the knockers on Miss?" Dave has the biggest grin on his face. Ola gives an immediate and sure-fire answer.

"Are you joking or what? Even Stevie Wonder's eyes would pop out at those things!"

Miss Goodyear teaches English and Drama. She's also one of the younger teachers, but more noticeably, the only female teacher at the lower school. She holds the boys' attention with her beauty, and this is more effective than any other teacher's technique. Even if Mr Solomon pointed a shotgun at the boy's, he wouldn't get their attention the way Miss Goodyear can.

Her long lashes frame her sparkling blue eyes, and this enchants the boys. Every time she moves, her brunette hair bounces and sways. Shanti thinks. *'She could be advertising shampoo, like the models on the telly.'*

When she smiles, she reveals her perfect teeth, and it disarms the boys. Without exception, every boy agrees that she's the best-looking woman at school. But there isn't any real competition. The only other women they see, are the dinner ladies, and most of them have bad teeth, and even worse figures.

Drama is compulsory until the boys reach the third year. Most of them don't take it seriously. They see it as an extended break. For two official hours a week, it lets them escape the inflexibility of their other lessons.

Miss Goodyear splits her class based on two factors. First, those with a shred of acting and performing ability. And second, those who are as dull in their imagination and dramatic skills, as an empty box. Despite taking in her every word, Shanti's in the second category. Throughout her lessons, he listens. The sound of her voice captivates him. And he watches every expression on her face.

He enjoys seeing the bridge of her nose wrinkle when she laughs. When she gestures with her hands, it's so passionate, she could be conducting an orchestra. Most of all. He loves her animated teaching style, which is in total contrast to others. The truth is, Miss Goodyear is Shanti's first crush.

Drama lessons also gives him a chance to let off steam. But through debates, Miss Goodyear makes him aware of their world.

"Boys, it's important to watch the news, or read a decent newspaper. Doing Ihis, will give you the best view of your world." Shanti follows her advice without any prompting. While watching the news, he asks.

"Abba, does the news only show horrible things?" Abba chuckles.

"Not always Baba. But right now, there're so many bad things happening. So many problems. It makes me worry about the future, but my education has helped me to get through tough times. That's why education is so important. If you get a good qualification, it will make you problem proof, and let you choose what you want to do." Shanti listens and thinks. *'As always, Abba can turn a simple answer into a lecture on education.'*

Through the media, he can see, that all these problems lead to a steady rise in racism. Every week there's another story about a racially motivated attack. Even at school, they have racists. There's Michael Anderson, who everyone calls Micky. In Micky's group, there's Ed and Steve, and with their reputation for bullying, racism becomes their natural home.

The rumours surrounding Micky sets the boys imagination on fire. According to the gossip, his entire family are racists, and his dad is canvassing for the National Front. None of them know the truth, but by the time the boys finish their character assassination, Micky's Dad is the Grand Wizard of the Ku Klux Klan!

Nat and Micky hate each other. They had a major bust up, a few weeks after starting school. Nat never told his friends what happened, but his hatred is still alive. In the playground, Nat lets his friends know his feelings.

"That Micky, more like pricky! Him and his family are scum! Why doesn't the school expel him? Bloody hell! They'd expel us if we did half the stuff him and his mates get up to!"

This is the first time they see Nat's anger. Not knowing what to say, the boys sit in silence. They wait for Nat to calm down, but Dave needs to have his say.

"Yeah, and Micky called me a Paki lover. I'd be alright if I knew what a Paki is." They're all amazed, and Shanti stutters.

"Dave, you're taking the piss. You telling me, you don't know what a Paki is?" Dave is adamant.

"I swear on my dog's life?" Shanti cannot believe his ears.

"Dave, now I know your winding me up. Cos you ain't even got a dog! Don't forget, I've been to your house."

Dave fires back.

"I only got the dog two days ago! So there! It's an Alsatian pup, he's bloody lovely, and I've called him Bumcrack!"

In an instant, the mood changes from bad temper, to laughing hysteria. The stupidity of the name has Shanti in tears of joy. Baldev nearly knocks his own turban off, while Ola holds his stomach, and tries to catch his breath. Once the laughter subsides, Shanti puts his arm around Dave's shoulder, and asks the question which is on everyone's lips.

"Bloody hell mate! How did you come up with that name?" After another outburst of laughter, Shanti adds.

"I tell you what. You tell us how your dog got that name, and I'll tell you what a Paki is."

It's a struggle to get everyone quiet, especially Nat, who sounds like he's having an asthma attack. They choke back their laughter, and Dave explains.

"I wanted a dog for years, and finally Dad gives in. He reckoned I'm old enough to look after a dog. So, we goes to Battersea Dogs home, and I picked out the one I wanted. When we got it home, Mum says, what you gonna call it? I didn't know. I couldn't think of a name. Well, on Sunday after dinner, Dad went upstairs to have a lie down, cos he'd had two helpings o' dinner, and a pudding. The dog was getting in the way, and Mum told Dad to take the dog with him. After I'd finished drying the dishes, I went upstairs to see if the dog was alright. Dad was flat out on the bed, and the dog was lying on his arse.

I think the dog was dreaming. So, I called Mum, and I asked. Can I call it Bumcrack, cos it's asleep on Dad's arse? Mind you, I had to beg her, but in the end, she gives in. She said I had to call it something else when Nan 'n' Granddad come over. But I'm sure Nan wouldn't mind, cos she swears like a bleeding trooper."

The boys listen, and the laughter stops. What at first sounded ridiculous, suddenly makes perfect sense. Now it's Shanti's turn to explain.

"Alright mate. I just can't wait for you to 'ave kids, God knows what you gonna call em! Right, the word Paki is short for Pakistani. Which means someone's from Pakistan, or for brown people, like Baldev and me. It's a bad word. It's like calling a black geezer, nigger, or like someone calling you, a wanker." Shanti watches Dave's face as he takes this in, but he doesn't understand.

"I've never heard anyone being called that, and Dad works with loads o' people on the docks. He always calls brown people Asian, and black people African. Anyway, Baldev's family are from Africa, so he can't be a Paki?"

Baldev smiles, he looks at Dave with kindness and answers.

"Mate, we're Ugandan, and we come to England from Uganda, a country in Africa. Cos I'm brown, people call me Paki."

Dave scratches his head.

27

"So, is Uganda near Pakistan then?" Baldev breaks into a big smile, at his friend's innocence.

"No mate, it's nowhere near, it's just coz I'm brown. It wouldn't matter where I was from. While I'm this colour, some people call me Paki."

Dave thinks about this, but he can't accept it.

"That's stupid. How can you call all brown people Paki? That's like calling all white people arseholes. Everyone's different. Blimey, Shanti you look nothing like Baldev, and you don't even come from Pakistan!"

They didn't have an answer, but they think about Dave's response. Shanti always thought that all white people knew and used this word. He remembers the first time someone called him Paki. He was seven years old, and only knew a few English words. Petrified and crying, he held Rani's hand, and they ran home.

"Ma, big boys called me Paki! They scared me." He said between sobs. Ma sat him on her knee, and Abba cuddled Rani.

"Oh Baba, Paki means bird in Bengali. They were calling you a little bird. Because you're so sweet. But if you see those boys again, come home straight away."

Shanti is sad that Ma told a lie, just to protect him.

Hearing Dave's words, hope surges through Shanti's heart. He realises that not all white people are racist, and his so-called stupid friend taught him this lesson.

The final lesson on Friday is Drama, and for Shanti it's the perfect way to start the weekend. Unless they're rehearsing for a school play, there's no structure. Miss Goodyear's syllabus consists of improvisations, and today is no exception. She decides to pair the boys. And deliberately, she mixes the races, and she explains.

"Boys, I want you and your partners to take the next few minutes to choose a topic. After the five minutes, each pair will debate and argue their chosen subject. You can choose anything, but it cannot be rude. You can choose football, religion, politics, where you live, and even the school. Okay?"

The boys respond, "Yes Miss." But Shanti isn't sure this is one of her best ideas. He knows that other teachers never allow them to debate, let alone argue. Miss Goodyear explains the purpose of the exercise.

"There are two simple rules. One, no swearing, and two, no interrupting one another. You must listen to your partner, and then you can speak. There's a fine line between an argument and a debate, and I want you to manage both." She then calls out the partners. Shanti waits, and then Miss Goodyear announces.

"Sadan, Anderson, you'll work together."

Shanti's thoughts explode. *'Micky Anderson, the king of the racists! No fucking way! It's impossible!'* For the first time he hates drama, and when he looks at Micky, he sees a cocky grin. Their eyes lock like two gunfighters ready to kill. Despite the visible hatred between them, Miss Goodyear appears oblivious, and carries on.

She pairs Nat and Dave without realising, they're good friends. When it's their turn, the best they can do is giggle, and this is infectious. Within thirty seconds, all the boys are laughing, and Miss Goodyear ends their performance.

"Time's up boys. I think I've seen more than enough. You two aren't taking this seriously, but I'll give you a C."

As soon as she grades them, they start arguing. Although neither of them cares about Drama, they still want Miss Goodyear to like them.

Dave shouts at Nat.

"It's your fault! You're just standing there like a lemon!"

This makes Nat angry.

"You can walk home by yourself. I'm not a lemon! You are!" There's a chorus of "oohs." And then there's more laughter. Their conviction impresses Miss Goodyear, and she changes her original C to a B, and this ends the argument. It's now Shanti and Micky's turn.

"Okay Sadan, Anderson, off you go. And remember the rules. Please pay particular attention to. No swearing."

The tension hangs in the air, like a thick black cloud. And the hateful stares increase. Now, Miss Goodyear notices, and she repeats the rules. But the boys don't make a sound, and they continue to stare at one another with hatred. During the preparation time, they ignored each other. Although it's only been ten seconds, for them, it feels like hours. Miss Goodyear breaks the deadlock.

"Come on boys, there must be one topic. How about football? Are you interested in football?" They nod.

"Okay, why don't you debate who's the better footballer, Kevin Keegan or Pele."

Shanti can't believe her choice and thinks. *'Bloody hell, these must be the only two players she's ever heard of.'* To him there's no comparison. He knows, Pele had been to four world cups and won three of them, and he'd scored over one thousand goals. He wonders whether Keegan will even come close to this tally. As he debates all of this in his head, Micky punctures the air with his opening line.

"Pele's like all black players, he's lazy and ignorant."

The audience gasp, and despite the initial shock, Shanti understands what ignorant means. Abba has called him that. He feels the full force of Micky's words, and his blood starts to boil, but he tries to stay calm. He stares at Miss Goodyear, and he pleads with his eyes. *'Miss, please stop this.'* When she doesn't, his calmness evaporates, and in its place, is seething anger.

"You and anyone else, who thinks that, must be ignorant. Pele was good enough to win three world cups, and he could beat any player put in front of him, black or white. He could dance rings round Keegan."

All the boys watch and listen. They expect a fight, but Micky stays calm.

"My brother Carl says. That all black people have smaller brains than whites, and they're no cleverer than monkeys."

He spits out the words, and they land on Shanti like bullets.

Miss Goodyear puts her hand over her mouth, and her eyes widen, but still, she allows it. Shanti sees Ola and Nat squirming, and now he responds with more hate.

"Oh yes, your brother Carl! I heard he can't even read or write. What does he know about football? Has he ever read a newspaper? Can he read one?"

Shanti meets Micky's vocal punches with his own poisonous words. He's sure Miss Goodyear will stop it now. Since he's attacked Micky's family. It's no longer about football, and they are close to violence.

Micky's face reddens, and he clenches his fists. Shanti's friends see this and sit up in their chairs, in case things get nasty. Shanti knows he has to make the peace. He thinks about Abba. When Abba is in a good mood, he is calm, gentle, and approachable. Shanti softens his tone.

"It doesn't matter what your brother thinks. Mickey, what do you think?"

He stares at Micky. He doesn't flinch, and then he sees the redness leave Micky's face. Everyone relaxes, and the tension eases. Micky looks at the floor, and he responds in the same soft tone.

"I suppose he's not a bad footballer for a black bloke, and I guess you don't win a world cup, if you're crap."

Shanti looks at his shoes, but it isn't because of fear. This time, he feels courageous, and it feels like a victory. He got a racist like Micky, to admit, that there's at least one good black man. This isn't easy, and outside school, it's impossible.

Silence and yawning follow their act. It's far too dull, and for the boys, the ending is an anti-climax. A voice from the back of the classroom sings out. "Boring!"

The boys stand motionless, unsure of Miss Goodyear's reaction. And when she nods, they walk back to their seats. Shanti looks over at Micky, and he returns the look with a fleeting smile. A gesture, that only ten minutes ago, was unimaginable.

Shanti returns the smile with caution, but somehow this victory feels hollow. He knows that in the outside world, where the school rules don't exist, it's meaningless. Racists and bullies didn't wait for someone to finish. Sometimes they didn't even wait for a person to start. He remembers looking at an older boy in the high street, and the boy screamed at him. "What you fucking looking at! You smelly Paki bastard!" Outside these walls, a mistimed glance is all it takes for violence to erupt. Miss Goodyear's enthusiastic outburst punctures Shanti's thoughts.

"A+! Well done boys. Very well done! My God, you had me worried, but the recovery was fabulous and worth the wait. You two will definitely have to audition for the Christmas play!" Miss Goodyear gives them a dazzling smile.

Whether she realises this or not, this wasn't an act. It was as real as the rules allow. Playing this out in a Christmas panto, would cause a riot. Shanti knows that this exercise balanced on a knife-edge, and had it gone wrong, Miss Goodyear would've lost her job. His overheard conversation between Mr Solomon and Mr Owen confirms this notion.

Once Miss Goodyear has the boys' attention, she explains the point of the lesson.

"Boys, try to remember that swearing or being offensive, always tips a debate into an argument. You should avoid this. Otherwise, it can end in violence, and this creates even more hatred, and it achieves nothing."

She stops and looks at the boys.

"To achieve a peaceful outcome, as Sadan and Anderson did, you must be firm, and flexible. It's important not to be insulting. At the start, you two were very insulting, and before you leave, I'd like you to shake hands. What impressed me was the way you turned it around. And that's being flexible. Do you know that some people love to hate? It's true, and when you show hatred in return, it fuels them, and makes them even more hateful. But if you can take away the anger, it can stop them. The real problem is. Many people have little self-control, and under pressure, they'll do and say anything. Even tell outright lies. The easiest thing is to walk away, but you may choose to confront it. Either way, stay calm. It's difficult and it takes practise. Now, any questions?"

Most of the boys just stare. Miss Goodyear's words confuse them, but Shanti hangs on to her every word. He notices that Micky, is doing the same. And while she's still beautiful, for Shanti, her beauty is now secondary.

He doesn't understand the entire message, but he feels different. Something penetrates his mind, and he's certain that it's done the same for Micky. Miss Goodyear manages to imprint some new ideas on them.

Outside the classroom, Dave sums up what many feel.

"What a load o' bollocks! What was she on about! How you gonna fight someone with a load o' words, and how you gonna keep talking, when some fucker kicks your teeth in? We should do boxing or Kung Fu, so we can beat the shit out of these wankers!" He grins, and then carries on.

"I heard o' some Japanese bloke, his names something like Demura. This bloke can kill you with his bare feet. Bloody hell, that's a bit special!"

"With your bloody feet you don't need Kung Fu! You could just kill 'em with the smell!" Nat follows this with a friendly headlock.

While Shanti laughs, he's still thinking about Miss Goodyear's words. He feels proud of the A+. It's his first, but he knows it won't impress Abba. Abba gave his opinion of drama, after seeing his planner.

"What's the point? They should cancel it and give you extra maths. You'll learn nothing in these stupid classes!"

As the weeks pass, Shanti sees the gradual changes in Micky. Micky no longer harasses him, or his friends, and he knows, Abba is wrong.

He still struggles, to understand why people feel such anger and hatred. But the most confusing part for him. Is Abba's anger, and he wonders. *'What's making Abba so mad?*

A Muslim Boy - Tolerance

"13 young black people dead in a house fire during a birthday party in New Cross!" This devastating tragedy dominates the newspaper headlines, and television reports.

Shanti lives five miles from New Cross, and the 53 bus he takes to school, stops outside the burned down house.

Rumours are rife, and many people suspect, a racially motivated arson attack, and this causes even more tension. From their actions, or lack of actions, the police appear gutless. Also, there's little sympathy from many white people in the area.

In January, Shanti decides to go to the West End, to find a bargain in the sales. He also wants to have a look at the remains of 439 New Cross Road. His morbid curiosity gets the better of him.

At the town centre, three skinheads board the bus. Shanti is sitting upstairs with half a dozen passengers. They're all minding their own business. He thinks nothing of it, until one skinhead sits next to him. He knows this means trouble, since three quarters of the seats are empty. He stares out of the window. He tries his best to ignore the skinhead next to him. These skinheads aren't boys, they're full-grown men, and much bigger than him. Despite feeling scared, he stays calm.

When the skinhead next to him stands up, he takes the cigarette out of his mouth. And when the bus stops, he snarls.

"Thirteen down, plenty more to go!"

Shanti jerks his head back to the window. He grips the seat rail in front of him. The skinhead makes a sudden movement. And with pure hatred in his eyes, he pushes the cigarette onto Shanti's knuckle. He presses it hard. Shanti doesn't have time to move his hand away, and the pain is numbing, but he doesn't flinch. He turns his head and stares at the skinhead. The bus stops and the skinheads get off. From the pavement, the three look up at Shanti, and they give a defiant Nazi salute.

In a hurry, Shanti brushes the burning tobacco embers from his knuckle, and licks the wound. An old White Woman witnesses this vile act. She walks over and sits next to him.

"You alright love?" she asks with concern.

Her words make Shanti tearful, and he nods. She reaches into her handbag and takes out a tube of antiseptic cream, and a packet of tissues.

"Give it here. Let me have a look." She cleans the burn with one tissue, and then applies the ointment. She places a clean tissue over the burn and holds his hand.

"When you get off the bus, buy a plaster, and before you go to bed, take the plaster off. The air will help it heal."

Shanti acknowledges her words with a nod, and he takes a deep breath, to stop his tears.

"Son, did you know. During World War II, the British and Indian Army fought scum like that? We fought to free ourselves of Nazis. I'm so ashamed that we've bred our own. They're not British. They're not even human. They're just animals."

In silence, they hold hands, as the bus rolls on. When the woman arrives at her stop, Shanti turns to her.

"Thank you."

It's all he can say without choking, and when a tear escapes, she wipes it away, and smiles. It's the sincerest smile he's ever seen.

From the window, he watches her. He sees an elderly black man, and two mixed race teenagers give her a warm and loving embrace.

This is her family, and one by one, she kisses them. She looks up and waves. A warm glow rises in Shanti's chest, and for a while, he forgets the pain.

The Refugee

After my first novel, I learned a lot of lessons, and so writing the 2nd, was a little easier. I knew what I wanted to say, so I started to think of the characters, their purpose, and their personalities. And of course, I had the big picture secure in my mind.

I learned from my first novel. It was the details which could trip me up. And so, I had to be disciplined, and ensure I retained the elements which added to the story, and I took out things which could make the story confusing.

The motivation for this came from the goodbyes my family and I endured when we left Bangladesh, and I saw the pain on my Grandparents faces. I don't remember it clearly, but what I do remember, was watching my parents suffering.

While I was growing up, I remember speaking to friends about their departure from Libya, Uganda, and other places. And some of my friend's parents spoke about their departure from Egypt, during the Suez crisis. All of these people expressed one common feeling. The hurt they felt, for those they left behind.

And more recently seeing the news reports from Syria. There was one image that struck me, but due to copyright I cannot show it, but I can describe it.

It is of a man in Aleppo in Syria, perhaps in his 60's, perhaps much younger, but someone that has been aged through worry and heartache. He is sitting on a low brick wall. I see the devastation around him, and his clothes are covered in dirt. I don't know if his hair is grey, or it is just dust. The thing I notice most, is the suit he wears. From what I can tell, it was once a decent suit. Perhaps, a suit worn by a professional. But it has aged as badly as he has. He also wears a shirt, and his tie hangs loosely. This was once a man who took pride in his appearance. Then I see the hand holding the cigarette. I think I see a wedding band, but it's not clear.

I felt this was a man who had to say goodbye to his family, but the picture didn't give me any clues.

This image stayed with me, and thoughts of my grandparents, my parents, and all the people I had listened to, formed the basis of the story. What happens to those who get left behind?

On 31st October 2019 I released, The Refugee.

I hope you enjoy the three chapters, Departing, Alone, and Teaching.

The Refugee - Departing

It's the day that Naguib, Hassam and Samir will say goodbye to their children. Their emotions are raw, and not knowing when they'll see each other again, causes heartache without relief.

Hassam has borrowed an opened backed truck. While he, Naguib, and Samir sit in the cabin, everyone else sits on the cargo bed. As Anwar, Nawal, and Abdel look at the people, the streets, and the beige landscape. They all wonder if they'll ever see their country again.

Anwar thinks about all the days, he spent playing in this desolate place. He realises, that despite the heat, and the vastness of the desert that surrounds them, it doesn't erode the love they feel. If anything, it makes the love even stronger, because it can withstand the hostile and torturous climate.

At the harbour, Naguib and Hassam are busy with the suitcases. It allows them to hide their sadness from their children, but both men teeter on the edge of despair.

Samir cannot hold back her tears. And the only relief comes from the children's questions. Salma clutches Samir's hand, and then the children surround her.

"Don't cry Aunty. We'll come and visit you soon, and then you can come and visit us." Samir looks at Salma's beseeching eyes, and she gives her a tearful smile.

"Yes darling, and that will be a wonderful day." Nawal sits with Samir and the children, and when she speaks, her voice shakes with sadness.

"That's what you have to tell yourself Aunty. That at the end of this goodbye, there'll also be a hello." Although Nawal says this to comfort and reassure Samir, she wants to believe her own words.

Samir has the children close to her, and despite not having blood ties. From this day, there's a connection, and it creates an unbreakable bond.

As they wait, they hear an announcement over the crackly speakers, first in Arabic and then in English.

"Will all passengers please go to the departure area. Please make sure you have your passports, visas, and tickets. Anyone without these travel documents will not be allowed to board the ship…"

As the echoes of the announcement fade, they all stand up. The children still cling to Samir, and Samir hangs on to them. She needs their support more than they need hers.

All the adults listen as the children say goodbye to Naguib. They adore their grandfather, and while Farid sits on Naguib's lap, Rafa and Salma have their arms around him. Farid nuzzles into Naguib and asks.

"Jadd, will you come and live with us?" Rafa has a feeling it's unlikely, she seems to understand. Salma screams with excitement.

"Yes Jadd, come and live with us like now, and we can play together." Farid clenches his little fists, and cheers. It's breaking the adult's hearts. Naguib looks at all of them, and answers in a gentle voice.

"I will visit you in your dreams. Remember, when we're good, and Allah sees this, he makes our dreams come true. But you must be good, for that to happen."

Farid is fascinated.

"If you visit me in my dreams I'll never go to sleep. Because I'll wait for you, so that we can talk, and I can tell you about my new school."

Naguib squeezes Farid.

"You can write to me. So, it's important, that you learn to write. And when I get your letters, I'll write back." Rafa listens and then in a tearful voice, she speaks.

"Jadd, if you visit me in my dreams, I'll never wake up. I'll sleep and dream every day and night." Samir puts her hand over her mouth to stop herself from sobbing, but all the same, her body shakes with pent up tears.

Nawal and the children say their goodbyes. Anwar and Abdel linger a while longer. Abdel hangs his head, not with fear or shame, but with an overwhelming sense of loss. Hassam feels the same, but he holds back his sorrow.

"This is a new adventure for you, and it will challenge you. But remember where you came from." Abdel chokes back his tears.

"I'll never forget anything. You are my heart, and I hope my heart doesn't break without you."

Samir moves closer to her son.

"As with everything we lose, for a while we hurt, but after a time we learn to cope. Our heartbeat adapts to our new surroundings, and we get through. You'll get through, I know it, and every day you'll be in my prayers."

Abdel's head sinks even further, and Hassam supports him.

"Be strong my boy." Abdel puts his arms around Samir and Hassam's neck, and they hold onto their son. As they watch Abdel walk away from them, Hassam, and Samir's face sag. And in that moment, they look a hundred years older.

Anwar keeps his eyes locked on Naguib.

"I'll send for you Abbi."

Naguib doesn't look away, and then he asks.

"Do you remember what I said to you about leaving?"

"Yes Abbi, I remember."

Naguib summons all his strength and speaks.

"Let me remind you. Your future and all that you and your children can achieve in life, depends on leaving. So don't leave with a heavy heart, just understand that this is the right thing to do. Stay strong for your family, and always put them above everything else. I'm happy to have done what I can. You are everything I could have wished for in a son."

Father and son embrace, and whisper in each other's ears.

"I love you."

Without another word, Anwar turns and walks away without looking back. Naguib also turns away and walks towards Hassam and Samir. He sees their bodies withering with pain. Their eyes remain glued to the ship. They hope they'll see Abdel one more time. When Naguib reaches them, he puts his arms around them, and sweeps them away from this torture.

On the ship, Abdel gazes back at the shore, but Anwar only looks to the horizon. Anwar cannot look back, he knows, it will weaken him. While the two men are different in how they deal with this parting, they both feel the same love for their family and their country. They're both proud Arab men.

The Refugee - Alone

Hassam drops Naguib at home, but for the entire journey, none of them say a word. They're all silenced by sadness, and they reflect on the separation from their loved ones.

Outside Naguib's house, Hassam speaks.

"Naguib, come and stay with us. You're alone now. But you don't have to be."

Naguib rests his hand on Hassam's arm.

"Thank you my friend. I'll come and visit later. But right now, I want to straighten the house. Also, I need to figure out, what I do next." Hassam nods, and Samir gives a weak smile, but there's no joy in her eyes.

As Naguib locks the door, he steels himself, and then he turns around. The overwhelming emptiness brings him to his knees, and his tears flow.

An hour later Naguib wakes up. He realises, that he passed out. He knows it's due to the exhaustion, caused by many sleepless nights, and heart-breaking days. It's the dead of night, and with no one else in the house, he hears every sound. He slows his breathing and listens. A part of him is hoping to hear his grandchildren sleeping. He used to smile when he could hear Farid giggling in his sleep. He wonders. *'What was going on in Farid's innocent mind? I wish I had asked him what he was dreaming of. Why didn't I ask him?'*

It dawns on him, that he'll never know the answer to this question. And he may never really know his grandchildren. From this day on, there'll be no shared experiences. Whatever they're about to face, they'll face without him.

He looks around the front room, and he sees the newspaper that Anwar was reading the day before. He picks it up, and he sees some scribbled notes. He runs his fingers across the indents. He folds the paper, and places it in the centre of the room.

He goes to Anwar and Nawal's bedroom. The bed is made, but when he opens the wardrobe, he sees some clothes still hanging there. As the door swings open, some of the hanger's rattle and it breaks the silence. He gathers the clothes and puts them in the centre of the front room.

Naguib then walks into the small room where the three children shared a bed. His heart aches when he sees some of the toys they left behind. With tears streaming down his face, he piles them in a line on the bed. He finds a toy police car, a doll with a missing arm, bits of paper with drawings of flowers, and little notes. He looks under the bed, and there's a small pair of sandals, and a ball. Farid left his ball behind and Naguib thinks. *'He loves that ball. He will miss it.'*

He gathers all the tokens and remains of his family. He puts them in a neat pile. Then he brings out the small, battered suitcase and fills it. And finally, he places the newspaper on top. It's a way of remembering the day, although he doesn't need any reminders. He knows, he'll never forget the day, he said goodbye to his family.

As the sun rises, he opens the windows. He stares at the suitcase. He decides to put it away. He knows, it will be hard enough to remove the feelings of loss, but he doesn't want a constant reminder.

He makes himself tea, and then sits on the veranda. Looking across the yard, he shuts his eyes, and he remembers the sound of his grandchildren's laughter. During his daydream, there's a knock at the door. The sun has only risen, and he wonders. *'Who could it be?'*

When he opens the door, he's surprised to see his neighbour, Mrs Kulthum. She has a tray in her hand, and as soon as the door opens, she speaks.

"As-salaam-alaikum Mr Ghali."

"Wa-alaikum-salaam Mrs Kulthum. How are you, and what brings you here?" Mrs Kulthum hands Naguib the tray.

"I made food. But I made too much, so I thought, I'd share it with you."

Naguib smiles.

"Shukraan Mrs Kulthum, this is very kind of you." It's all he can say. Since his neighbour's kindness overwhelms him. Mrs Kulthum stares at Naguib's watery eyes.

"Mr Ghali, you don't have to sit on your own, please come and spend time with us."

Naguib blinks hard to stop the tears.

"I just need a little bit of time. From not having a space to think in, I now find I have too much space, and too many thoughts. I suppose that's Allah's blessing and curse. He gave humans time to feel, to think, and to reflect." With a gentle hand, Mrs Kulthum touches Naguib's arm.

"Whenever you're ready Naguib. Please call me Yousra." With those words, Yousra Kulthum breaks the barriers of formality, which have existed for decades.

"Thank you Yousra."

50

Naguib's words are sincere, and as he re-enters the house he feels blessed. He understands that the new rhythm of his life will involve his neighbours, as well as others like him. He knew of many who said goodbye to their loved ones, and now he understands the sadness he sees in them. He understands where that sadness comes from.

Through his pain, he learns another lesson. You can repair a broken family. But the time they lose, is gone forever, and nothing can bring it back.

The Refugee - Teaching

Naguib, Sultan and Hussein, along with fifty other civilians, volunteer to clear the area around Sultan's home. The army and police, provide another fifty men and supervise the operation. Sultan finds the senior police officer and asks.

"Sir, my home was here, and these were my neighbours. Sir, if I find something that belongs to me, may I take it? I'm not stealing." The police officer asks.

"What sort of things?" Sultan looks at the officer.

"Photos of me and my wife, and any salvageable books, I am a teacher. That's all, nothing of value to anyone else."

The police officer is a kind man.

"When you find the things you want, put them next to my car. Let me check them, and as long as it doesn't look like you're looting, which I doubt, you can take them." Sultan shakes the officer's hand.

"Shukraan Sir, may Allah bless you." The police officer smiles, walks away, and barks orders at his men.

Recovering the remains of dead bodies is harrowing, and the stench is far worse than before. Despite the men wearing masks, it's excruciating. The bodies have been in the baking sun for six days. And the smell is a combination of putrefied rotting flesh, human waste, rotten eggs, rotten cabbage, and a strong garlic like odour. When the men move a body, insects scurry away. While these insects are nature's clean up team, it makes the men's flesh crawl. The men also wear gloves, to protect them from the toxic chemicals the body releases after death. From a

52

distance, it breaks the men's hearts, but as they get closer, they feel revulsion. Some men cry as they carry out the work.

First, they have to recover the visible remains, including those of women and children. Afterwards the army slarts to remove the debris, and this is a slow process. When they expose another body, the men lift the remains, bag them, and put them on a truck.

The work goes on for two weeks, but the increasing shellfire makes it too dangerous, and they evacuate the area.

Sultan is sure they haven't recovered all the remains, even some of his closest neighbours are still missing. He says a silent prayer. *'Inshallah, you're all staying with family, and you're not under the rubble.'*

In the end, they manage to recover, three more photos, and a dozen books. But the most important thing for Sultan. Is the chance to say goodbye to his neighbours, and to pray for their souls.

It takes Sultan nearly two months to adjust to his new surroundings. He suffers with bad dreams, and sometimes they turn into nightmares. Zeina often sits in his room and fans him. Sometimes she hums a tune to sooth him, in the same way she sings lullabies to her children, to help them sleep.

Slowly Sultan appears to be his old self again, but for the rest of his life, he carries a deep unhealed wound. Naguib had known the young, vibrant, and humorous Sultan, and he can see that less than half his vigour and strength has survived. He puts part of the change down to old age. But in his heart, he knows, Sultan will never be the same again, since grief and loss has robbed a big part of his character.

As they sit on the veranda, Naguib asks.

"When do you want to start teaching? Hussein told me that he has the space for a classroom, on the roof of his house. He has a large piece of tarpaulin, and it will shade you and your students from the sun." Sultan is in a thoughtful mood.

"I'll need something to write on, a blackboard if we can get one. I'll also need, some chalk, pencils, exercise books, and a few other things?" Naguib looks at Sultan.

"Make a list of the things you need, and I'll make sure you get it. A blackboard might be difficult, but what if we paint the bricks black, would that work?" Sultan thinks about it.

"I suppose it would, I don't see why not. Let's try that first. Naguib, I don't have much money, but please take it. I need to do this. Sitting around doing nothing, is turning me into a vegetable. Sometimes we have too much time to think." Naguib agrees.

"Yes, you're right. It's both a blessing and a curse to have brains that remember. Don't worry about the money. There are many children in the neighbourhood, who could do with the extra help. I'm sure their parents will give what they can. We'll manage."

Naguib, Hussein, and Sultan build the classroom. They secure the tarpaulin to the wall with wooden batons, and Naguib builds a frame and secures the tarpaulin to it. The neighbours bring things that might be of use, including an old rug that has seen better days. Yousra stares at it with a frown.

"Why are you bringing that flea bitten thing into my house? Hussein answers.

"It's for the classroom." Yousra shakes her head, and then inspects the rug for a full ten minutes. When

54

she's satisfied that there are no bugs living in it, she gives her begrudging approval.

"Alright, take it to the roof, but don't touch anything in the house with this piece of junk."

After three days of sifting through rubbish, the charity of neighbours and anyone willing to help, the classroom is ready.

It's a large space, and it takes up half the roof, or around twenty square metres, enough for fifteen to twenty students at a squeeze.

The adults gather on the roof. Sultan is humbled by the occasion, and with his chin quivering, he speaks.

"I'd like to live here, and I'd like to make this space my home. I should always be here for the students. Anyone wishing to learn should never have to look for me." With raised eyebrows, Naguib looks at the others.

"Sultan, this isn't meant to be a permanent room, there's a tarpaulin roof, and it'll keep the sun off you, but that's it. There's one solid wall and two canvas sides. It's more like a tent than a permanent structure." Sultan answers.

"Our Bedouin brothers live in tents, why can't I?" Naguib doesn't have an answer.

"Very well, but I'll have to make all the sides covered, and with something a little stronger. I'll also have to add a flap, so you can open and shut it. It will keep out flies and mosquitoes." Sultan listens, and nods.

"Shukraan Naguib. Hussein, Yousra, do you have any objections to me living on your roof. I'll pay you rent. Please don't answer that while I'm standing in front of you, think about it and let me know." Hussein already knows the answer.

"I'll answer you now. When you first came here, I said, you could stay with us, and I haven't changed my mind. I just didn't expect you to live on the roof like a flying gypsy, but if you're happy to do this, we're happy to call this your home. Please don't worry about rent, get yourself sorted."

Sultan smiles.

"I want to thank all of you for your generosity. Your kindness breaks my heart, but some heart breaks are good."

This is Sultan's new home, a makeshift Bedouin tent on the roof of Yousra and Hussein's house. Everyone helps to make it as cosy as possible. There's a small bed, a desk, a chair, a bookshelf, and the threadbare rug for the students to sit on. On the bookshelf are the photos Sultan managed to recover. He positions them in a way, so that he can see Rania when he's in bed. Every night while he sleeps, Rania watches over him.

During the day, he teaches the children. He starts with Gamal and Hanan, and sometimes he teaches adults, since many want to learn English. For them, it's a possible escape route. There are no fixed fees, and people give whatever they can. Sultan gives the money to Yousra, who at first refuses it, but realises, it's easier to accept it. Then she gives the money to Naguib, and he uses it to buy what Sultan needs, and gives Sultan the change, along with a made-up excuse.

"One of the parents gave me this money to give to you. I can't remember the name, but she said her daughter, or is it her son, is enjoying school."

Sultan teaches everyone who comes to him. He doesn't discriminate, and he welcomes anyone who wants to learn.

On clear and quiet nights, Sultan sits on the roof gazing at the stars. Neighbours who sit on their roofs to feel the cool evening air, wave to him. The people in the neighbourhood call him the Bedouin teacher, a title he carries to the end of his days.

On those starlit nights, Sultan speaks to Rania.

"My beautiful Rania, I will see you soon."

Mercurius – Slavery

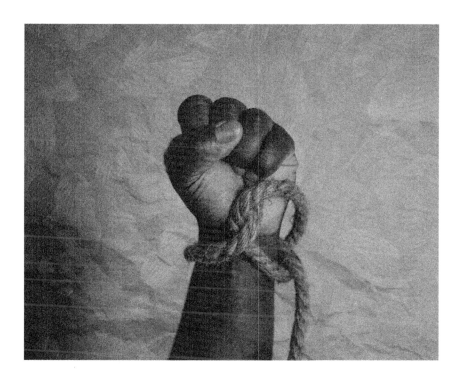

I wrote this article a few months after the death of George Floyd. He was murdered on May 25, 2020, in the U.S. city of Minneapolis by Derek Chauvin, a 44-year-old white police officer.

This caused me a lot of pain, and I wanted to say something about this incident, but highlight another fact. This isn't a one off.

At the time, I was approached by an online magazine, Mercurius, and I submitted this article, and they ran it.

Slavery - Article

George Floyd's death has massive and tragic consequences, but in the U.S.A there have been many other black men, who have died at the hands of the police. Ahmaud Arbery in 2020, Freddie Gray in 2015, and Eric Garner in 2014 to name a few. Let's not sit back and say this is an American problem, it isn't. In Britain, in 2019 Simeon Francis died in police custody, Sheku Bayoh in 2015, and Mikey Powell in 2003. This is the tip of the iceberg. There are many more incidents such as these.

Capturing footages of injustice is a good thing. It helps people become aware of those injustices. It allows people to ask, are the police fit to do their jobs? From what we see and read, there's a handful that obviously aren't, and this leads to death. It also asks many other questions. Are the forces themselves flawed, how are they trained, what motivates them, and are those in charge of policing the police, truly independent?

Growing up in Southeast London during the 70's and 80's, I experienced racism and violence. I grew up three miles from where Stephen Lawrence was murdered. I've asked myself. Where does racism come from? It's a tough question, and there are many people better qualified to answer this. So, I will tell you what I believe.

I believe racism stems from ignorance and fear. As Gandhi once said. *"The enemy is fear. We think it is hate; but it is really fear."*

All people fear things they don't understand or trust. It can be fear of deep water or flying, or it can be the fear of another race or religion, but with education all fears can be overcome. I've travelled extensively and found good people everywhere. However, I've met a handful of people, who asked me questions about the British society. Their ignorance made them believe that all Brit's were immoral. I pointed out. How does a society survive if it's as immoral as you say it is?

I believe ignorance and fear equals hatred. History has proven this. Six million dead Jewish people proved this with their lives, and millions more who have died due to ethnic cleansing.

Does slavery still exist? Of course it does. Have a look at the stories about illegal immigrants who enter the U.S. or Britain. And these are just two countries. Think of the football stadiums that have been built in Qatar, for the World Cup, on the back of cheap labour. Think of the sweatshops around the world.

These immigrants are often enslaved by those who bring them into the country. They are not free. Many live in dire conditions, while others turn to crime, or are forced into prostitution. Their minds and spirits are enslaved.

Bob Marley's lyrics in Redemption song says. *"Emancipate yourself from mental slavery."* I would ask the question. How do you emancipate yourself from mental slavery, if those put in power to protect you, feel like the enemy? Mental slavery for many, also comes in the form of debt. They are shackled by what they owe. The treadmill of debt stifles lives, and in many cases it erodes our biggest asset, our imagination. To dream, hope, genuinely smile, live in the present, and aspire. Which to me, is our best medicine. Debt can destroy all of those healing human qualities.

With every death such as George Floyd, we open old wounds. We nurture fear, we create mistrust.

In 1963 Martin Luther King Jr said. *"I have a dream that my four little children will one day live in a nation where they will not be judged by the color of their skin, but by the content of their character."*

I wonder if more than half a century after that speech, we are still asking the same questions.

This poem looks at slavery of yesterday and today.

Slavery – Poem

African, Asian and Global Slaves,
Never have the chance to be brave,
Their lives are torn apart,
Families destroyed, broken hearts,
Fathers, sons, mothers gone,

Taken from the love they came from.

Brought to foreign lands in crowded ships,
Food in tiny ration, stagnant water they sip,
Abuse, floggings, murder, and rape,
Hidden, silenced, only death gives an escape,
History tried to hide the truth,
Hidden under the grand slave trader's roof.

The modern slave trader drives a Bentley,
And they talk ever so gently,
They are the epitome of a businessman,
The government praises their business plans,
They may be knighted or become a dame,
The government takes absolutely no blame.

Does slavery still exist?
Yes, the way the police persist,
Profiling and brutal enforcement of laws,
Police attitudes have too many flaws,
The government talks a good fight,
But are they sympathetic of the plight?

Equality is the only way,
You can shake off mental slavery and say,
I am free to be who I want to be,
I am not offending anyone, can't you see,
Freedom to choose has always been mine,
It is the one rule we should enshrine.

Governments be brave and do the right thing,
Erase statues and memorials that sting,
You are in power to represent all,
Don't leave behind those who fall,

Rewrite history with truth and bravery,
Try to remove the pain caused by slavery.

Mercurius - Cultural Slavery

This was the second article I wrote for Mercurius magazine, and it follows the slavery theme. But this time I wrote it from a more personal perspective.

My family started life in Britain as refugees, and so we had to change. Despite trying to hold onto some traditions, the change was inevitable.

Cultural Slavery - Article

As a British Asian who arrived in England at the age of seven, I have asked myself, where do I belong? It is not easy to answer this question, even for those who never leave their place of birth. Where you live, and the culture that surrounds you, will affect you. It will shape your opinions and thinking, until you are also part of the cultural identity of that place.

Some people call that good citizenship, and I suppose from a law-abiding standpoint, this is true. However, I wonder if this also creates injustice and inequality. Does it create a need to hide your true self? I don't know the answer to this, and the debate is far bigger than this article.

Like many people, I watch television, and I watch the adverts. If you are unfortunate enough to be a bit of an insomniac, you will know that late night television is full of ads. These ads tell us what we need in our lives, and it is anything from a miracle-cleaning product, all the way to a Russian diver's watch. Unless you are a Russian diver, I don't think you really need the watch.

My concern is. Does the media, with all its power try to define us? I can see from these ads, that it tries to sell the idea, that we all need the same things to make us happy. Through these ads, many of which are global, the subliminal message is, buy this product and you will be part of something bigger. Let us call it, a flattening of the cultural divide through retail. Surely, we cannot all need the same things. A person in New York or London will buy a water filter for his taps, or faucets, while a person in an African or Indian village, simply needs clean water.

Then I asked. Does an untouchable Hindu have the same cultural aspirations as a Brahmin, a high-class

Hindu? Even if they did, would the Hindu culture allow an untouchable to climb the social and career ladder? My feeling is. The Hindu culture might be too stuck in its ways to allow change.

The Chinese civilization, to our knowledge, is over 3000 years old. This nation had a culture that survived right up until Puyi, the last emperor left the Forbidden City, in 1924. That is not to say the culture was right or fair. The following thought crossed my mind. Are the Chinese right in trying to recreate China in the image of the west? Currently there are more than 60 million empty properties, and 50 ghost towns in China. Most Chinese people cannot afford to live in these places, and I wondered if they would prefer to live a simpler village life, rather than in these high-rise cities.

I believe that supressing a culture can be as damaging as having a culture, which does not yield and represses people.

On 9th October 2012, a gunman shot Malala Yousafzai, as she rode home on a bus after an exam in Pakistan. She was 15 years old when a gunman shot her. This took place, because a young Pakistani girl wanted an education, something as basic as education created a cultural rift. Malala Yousafzai is a Nobel Prize winner, and she is able to stand up for what she believes. However, I wonder how many women die because they have stepped over the cultural rules of their society.

The bigger question is. How many people in the world feel enslaved or trapped by their culture? I ask myself, does culture create more barriers than it removes. In many ways, I think it does. These barriers live and grow in our minds, and our cultural fears nourish them and shape our thinking.

There is good and bad in all cultural identities, and as intelligent people, we have to decide what defines us, and what we are happy to accept without feeling guilty. To follow the rules of a culture with blind faith is to create intolerance, a lack of new ideas, and ultimately, live a life of cultural slavery.

This short poem tries to express the key elements of this article.

Cultural Slavery - Poem

Arrive in England in the chill of winter,
The cold feels like a sub-zero splinter,
The lights at Heathrow shine bright,
My frozen face only shows fright.

London is full of strange places,
People wrapped up, cold grey faces,
Frost twinkles and dances on the street,
The icy cold penetrates my feet.

Years go by and I adapt,
The culture doesn't feel apt,
Who am I in this place?
I fit in, but I feel no grace.

Twilight TV plays on my screen,
Do I really need this skin cream?
Should I buy a reclining chair?
What's wrong with the one I have here?

I am an untouchable waiting in line,
I can do the job. I hope I'll be fine,
Young man, your name is Harijan?
I am sorry but the job has gone.

Chinese farmer sits on the sixth floor,
There's no greenery outside his door,
I miss the warm embrace of my fields,
Concrete surrounds me like riot shields.

I am a girl I want to learn,
My own money I want to earn,
Is it wrong to want to read?
Why was I shot, why did I bleed?

Does culture try to define all of us?
Why is there so much fear and fuss?
Wait for cultures to become kind and calm,
Then we can stop the hurt and harm.

Mercurius - Financial Slavery

This was the final piece I wrote around the theme of slavery for Mercurius. And it looks at how money enslaves us.

Financial Slavery - Article

Debt is as much a pandemic as any virus because it touches so many. It's estimated that 75% of the world is in debt. Global debt reached $255 trillion in 2019, and in 2008 the time of the global financial crisis, debt was at $97 trillion. In twelve years, debt had increased by 163%.

This is a phenomenal increase in a very short space of time. On the web site, *This is Money* there is an inflation calculator. I chose the year 2007 and entered a value of £100, to see its value today. The answer it gave was £145.94. This is a 45% rise, but when we look at the rate debt has grown, its more than three times that increase. Therefore, debt increases faster, than we can repay it.

One of the key factors behind the crash of 2008 was the availability of cheap credit, and this turned into toxic debt. This toxic debt was due to irresponsible lending. People with no ability to repay their loans were given loans by companies, whose only criteria was to secure the loan, irrespective of the person's ability to repay the debt.

This mind-set of easy money still exists today. The sharp rise in debt says that we haven't learned any lessons. It's easy to run up debts. Buy now pay later, pay day loans and other financial instruments allow people access to easy money. For some debt starts at birth, it's the cost of medical bills.

In 2019 Lorie Konish wrote an article, and this is a very small segment. *'Research shows that about 137.1 million Americans have faced financial hardship this year because of medical costs.'*

For many, life starts with debt, and it follows individuals and their families throughout their lives. American students alone owed about $1.5 trillion in student loans at the end of March 2019, more than two times what they owed a decade earlier. In the U.K. during 2017/18 the value of student maintenance loans was £5.2b. But the hidden costs of these schemes and loans are horrifying, and like all debt, it has to be paid back, and that's when easy money becomes the slave master.

Recently I saw an ad offering a pay day loan with an interest rate of 1297%. This is an astronomical rate and one you might associate with a loan shark, and so I searched the internet, and this is what I found on Wikipedia.

"The research by the government and other agencies estimates that 165,000 to 200,000 people are indebted to loan sharks in the United Kingdom... Payday loans with high interest rates are legal in many cases, and have been described as "legal loan sharking."

It made me ask a couple of questions. Are we creating a new layer of toxic debt? Are we recreating another crash, but much bigger than 2008? I read a quote by Albert Einstein, and his definition of insanity was.

"Doing the same thing over and over again and expecting different results."

Financial problems are one of the biggest attributable factors in suicides. Debt can make a person feel hopeless, impulsive, aggressive, isolated, a failure and ultimately it could cause mental illness resulting in tragic consequences. Debt is financial slavery, and the rate that debt is growing, it's likely that most of us will be enslaved.

Debt is man-made slavery. The more debt grows, the more we are enslaved by it. Think of it as a way of silencing the masses. While we worry about debt, we don't really ask questions about those, who allow debt to grow in this exponential way.

I want to briefly look at a nation's debt, and I'll use Greece as an example. Before Greece could adopt the Euro in 2001, it had to reduce its debt levels, as part of the Euro adoption criteria. With the help of Goldman Sachs, Greece did this by re-profiling part of its debt as currency swaps. A currency swap is a foreign exchange transaction that involves trading principal and interest in one currency, for the same in another currency. The sleight of hand worked, Greece met the debt criteria and adopted the Euro. It soon became clear that the currency being traded had no real value, but by then Greece had the Euro.

After twenty years of taking on more debt, Greece has locked itself into a life of debt. On 30 June 2015, Greece became the first developed country that failed to make an IMF loan repayment on time. It needed another bailout, and another debt. The curse of debt for Greece will continue for many years, and there could be a couple of generations who pay the price for Greece's policies over the last 20 years. The austerity for the Greek people will continue.

And just like Greece, I think of those who are taking out their first payday loan, credit card, and signing up to a, buy now pay later scheme. It's easy to say, think again, and try to remember that debt is a spiral. The more you borrow, the more you become reliant on borrowing. The reality is, we are enticed on a daily basis by the media to achieve a certain lifestyle, and that often means getting into debt.

The worrying part about this is, we haven't considered the coming years. These could be the years that banks are broken. It's better for us to try and adjust while we have a choice.

I think during this pandemic, people have realised how little they need. I hope these lessons continue to serve us well, and we think twice before making another purchase on credit. Only to realise that we have no use for it, by which time the debt is incurred.

This is a short poem which tries to express the key elements of this article.

Financial Slavery - Poem

Mother stares at her baby with love,
Phone vibrates from the cupboard above,
Father receives a text from the bank,
What shall we call our boy Frank?

Father stares at his boy with a smile,
Father thinks, I'm out of credit, wait a while,
Father replies, anything you like,
Mother smiles, what about Mike.

The family manages to make ends meet,
The boy is embarrassed by the friends he greets,
Their clothes are trendy and new,
This is all I have, I have so few.

University starts, life is great,
Student loan agreed, parties negate,
The reality of the debt,
Cost of education is a sure bet.

Start working, pay back debts,
Cycle of debt creates regrets,
Buy now pay later says the ad,
Feel better, but the small print is bad.

Buy a house 25 years to pay,
25 years of debt, is that the way?
We all have to live this life,
It's easier to divorce your wife.

Take a policy to pay funeral costs,
Borrowing till our life is lost,
The cycle of debt enslaves,
Until our vision of life is in a cave.

Nations borrow to secure citizens,
Paying back, it's not pretty then,
Toxic loans crash the market,
Pay day loans create new toxic circuit.

Debts enslave people and ruin lives,
Politicians and bankers continue to thrive,
Will we learn to control our spending?
Not as long as someone is lending.

The Archer – Bernadine Evaristo

London Diaries – Bernadine Evaristo

This morning as I ate breakfast, I started to read about Bernadine Evaristo, or to use her full name, Bernardine Anne Mobolaji Evaristo. The reason I started to read about her was, she is to be the next president of the Royal Society of Literature, becoming the first writer of colour to hold the position, and only the second woman in the society's 200-year history.

Founded in 1820, the Royal Society of Literature describes itself as 'the UK's charity for the advancement of literature'. Evaristo will take over from historian Marina Warner as president at the end of this year.

Then I read about her, and I learned that she was born in Eltham, south-east London, and raised in Woolwich.

Woolwich! That's where I grew up. I went to Woolwich Polytechnic Secondary School for Boys. The school is still there. Despite our lives taking different paths, I somehow felt a connection. As far as I know, I haven't met her, but I realised that she saw the same things I saw. She walked along the same streets I did. She experienced some of the things I experienced, and she made it. I felt proud. I felt, it was a friend who achieved this.

I read about her family history, and I learned that she was the fourth of eight children born to an English mother, who was a schoolteacher. And a Nigerian father, Julius Taiwo Bayomi Evaristo (1927–2001), known as Danny. He was born in British Cameroon, raised in Nigeria. He migrated to Britain in 1949 and became a welder and the first black councillor in the Borough of Greenwich. I understood that her father raised the bar high, despite the bigotry that he must have faced. In those days England was not as tolerant as it is today, and there was no such thing as political correctness.

Evaristo was educated at Greenwich Young People's Theatre (formerly The Tramshed). As a young man, I visited the Tramshed, and I got a chance to see concerts, comedy shows, and plays.

I wondered. *'On those nights I was there, did I stand near, or next to her?'* I then wondered. *'Did I ever say hello to her, and did she say hello back to me?'* I'd love to think she did. This was over 35 years ago, and I can't remember. She probably looked different then, I know I did. For a start, my hair was jet black, but today, it is mostly grey.

This is what The Tramshed looked like back in the 70's and 80'S.

I learned that she attended Goldsmiths College, University of London, and she received her doctorate in creative writing in 2013. I knew this place as well. The 53 Bus I travelled on, stopped outside Goldsmiths.

She was appointed Woolwich Laureate by the Greenwich and Docklands International Festival.

I searched the Internet to see what were the upcoming events that she would be attending, and I came across the following.

"Bernardine Evaristo, Julian Barnes, and Deborah Levy are among the headliners for the 2022 Hay Festival.

At the time of writing this, Covid restrictions exist. I am hoping the restrictions wont scupper the event, and I will try to get tickets.

In the meantime, I am going to read her books. Her novel **The Emperor's Babe** is about a teenage black girl, whose parents are from Nubia. It won an Arts Council Writers' Award in 2000. A NESTA Fellowship Award in 2003, and it was chosen by The Times, as one of the 100 Best Books of the Decade in 2010.

Soul Tourists is about a mismatched couple driving across Europe to the Middle East, and it features ghosts of real figures from European history.

Blonde Roots is a satire that reverses the history of the transatlantic slave trade. It replaces it with a universe where Africans enslave Europeans. It won the Orange Youth Panel Award and Big Red Read Award. It was also nominated for the International Dublin Literary Award, and the Orange Prize and the Arthur C. Clarke Award.

Lara fictionalises the multiple cultural strands of her family history. It goes back over 150 years. It also looks at her mixed-race London childhood. It won the EMMA Best Novel Award in 1998.

Her novella **Hello Mum** was chosen as "The Big Read" for the County of Suffolk.

Her 2014 novel **Mr Loverman** is about a septuagenarian Caribbean Londoner, a closet homosexual considering his options after a 50-year marriage to his wife. It won the Publishing Triangle Ferro-Grumley Award for LGBT Fiction, and the Jerwood Fiction Uncovered Prize.

Her novel, **Girl, Woman, Other**, is an innovative "fusion fiction. " It is about 12 primarily black British women. Their ages span 19 to 93 and the novel charts their hopes, struggles and intersecting lives. In October 2019, it won the Booker prize jointly with Margaret Atwood's, The Testaments.

The win made her the first black woman and first black British author to win the prize. In 2020, Evaristo was recognised for her writing, as one of the United Kingdom's most influential people of African or African Caribbean heritage, by being included in the 2021 edition of the annual Power list.

And all this from a person that was almost a neighbour. Someone who visited the same places I visited, and their reality was the same as mine. And her words have inspired me.

'Struggle, positivity, vision, activism and self-belief have all contributed towards my unstoppability.'

Bernadino, we have never spoken, but it feels like, you are talking to me.

The Archer – Ernest Hemingway

London Diaries – Ernest Hemingway

Life slows down from 24th December to the New Year. It is the Christmas and New Year Holidays, and this year I received a collection of books by Ernest Hemingway. I have been fascinated with Hemingway and his style of writing since reading, The Old Man and The Sea. This was over twenty-five years ago.

I love the way the narrative immediately involves the reader. It was the first book I read without stopping. I couldn't put it down.

The story tells of an epic struggle between an old, seasoned fisherman, Santiago, and the greatest catch of his life, an 18-foot (5.5 meter) Marlin. And while the story ends in failure, it rekindles the bond between him and his devoted apprentice and friend, Manolin.

For me, the story tells of the struggles we all face, and it feels like a metaphor for life. We fight. Sometimes we win, and sometimes we lose, but in the end, those that are real friends, remain. Friends aren't bothered whether we win or lose, all a friend wants, is for us to be happy on the path we have chosen. All they ask is, we return to them.

As always, my fascination with someone, makes me inquisitive. Over the years, I learned a lot about Hemingway, but here is a brief piece, which gives an idea of him as a writer.

"Ernest Miller Hemingway (July 21, 1899 – July 2, 1961) was an American novelist, short-story writer, journalist, and sportsman. His economical and understated style—which he termed **the iceberg theory**—*had a strong influence on 20th-century fiction. Hemingway produced most of his work between the mid-1920s and the mid-1950s, and he was awarded the 1954 Nobel Prize in Literature. He published seven novels, six short-story collections, and two nonfiction works. Three of his novels, four short-story collections, and three nonfiction works were published posthumously. Many of his works are considered classics of American literature."*

I've highlighted the words, iceberg theory, since it is essential to his writing style, and this is the explanation.

"Hemingway said that only the tip of the iceberg showed in fiction—your reader will see only what is above the water—but the knowledge that you have about your character that never makes it into the story acts as the bulk of the iceberg. And that is what gives your story weight and gravitas."

Hemingway learned this style as a young journalist. He focused his reports on urgent events, and he didn't worry about their meaning. The event was everything. When he started to write short stories, he continued with this minimalistic style, focusing on the immediate elements without explicitly discussing underlying themes. Hemingway believed that the deeper meaning or morality of a story shouldn't be obvious, but it should shine through.

The following is a list of Hemingway's top ten books. The Sun Also Rises, A Farewell to Arms, The Complete Short Stories of Ernest Hemingway, By-Line, Death in the Afternoon, Three Stories and Ten Poems, Green Hills of Africa, For Whom the Bell Tolls, A Moveable Feast, and The Old Man and the Sea.

To me, his stories, reflect the battles he won and lost, and they shaped him, as events in our own lives shape us. Here are examples of some enormous events in Hemingway's early life, but there are many more.

In December 1917, Hemingway responded to a Red Cross recruitment drive. And he signed on to be an ambulance driver in Italy. On his first day in Milan, he joined rescuers to retrieve shredded remains of female workers. He describes the incident in his non-fiction book, Death in the Afternoon.

"I remember that after we searched quite thoroughly for the complete dead, we collected fragments."

I was shocked. Fragments! Amongst the stench, the debris, and destruction, just to find pieces of a body. I wondered. What does that do to a person? What does that do to someone so young? It is a brutal awakening, and the innocence of youth is forever lost.

In July, Hemingway suffered a serious injury by mortar fire. Despite this, he carried on, and was awarded the Italian Silver Medal of Military Valour. He was only 18, and later, he said.

"When you go to war as a boy you have a great illusion of immortality. Other people get killed; not you ... Then when you are badly wounded the first time you lose that illusion, and you know it can happen to you."

He then suffered severe shrapnel wounds to both legs. After an immediate operation, he was hospitalised. While recovering, he fell in love with Agnes von Kurowsky, a nurse who was seven years older than him. He believed Agnes would join him after his return to the U.S. and they would marry. Instead, he received a letter to say, she was engaged to an Italian officer. The rejection devastated and scarred him. In future relationships, Hemingway followed a pattern of abandoning a wife before she abandoned him. This explains why he married four times.

Despite the horrors Hemingway saw in Italy, I felt, the rejection was his real battle. And the combination of horror and heart ache, created the adult personality that would dominate his character. Back then, people didn't recognise conditions caused by the mental scars and trauma of conflict, such as Post Traumatic Stress Disorder, PTSD. This was only discovered in 1980. PTSD is characterised by disturbing thoughts about the incident, recurring distress and anxiety, flashbacks, and avoidance of similar situations. This can lead to alcohol or drug abuse, as a way of coping, or shutting out these thoughts. Hemingway chose alcohol.

The theme of death runs throughout Hemingway's work. But for me, it is not simply the death of a person. Reading his works, I realised that it is also the death of a way of life, something familiar, or something cherished. And we mourn all these things.

During his final years Hemingway suffered with depression. He behaved like his father, who killed himself in 1928. His father may have had hereditary hemochromatosis, where the excessive accumulation of iron in tissues, culminates in mental and physical deterioration. Medical records confirm that Hemingway was diagnosed with hemochromatosis in early 1961. His sister Ursula and his brother Leicester also killed themselves. There are other theories which try to explain Hemingway's decline, and this includes. The multiple concussions he sustained throughout his life, caused chronic traumatic encephalopathy, CTE. Despite receiving 20 gruelling rounds of electroconvulsive therapy, Ernest Hemingway shot himself in the head, two days after returning home from hospital.

I asked myself. Did his condition, along with alcohol, erode his intellect? To the extent, where the fear of losing his ability to write, to argue, and to make sense of things, was just too scary. I am sure the answer is yes. I think, rather than allow time to dictate the terms of his death, the erosion of his mind, body, and senses, he chose to act. As a writer, he wanted to have the last word.

These thoughts led me to see parallels in his life, with another person I consider a hero, Robin Williams. Williams was a sharp-witted comedian and actor. Many consider him as the sharpest wit for many generations. However, he suffered from lewy body dementia, a devastating and debilitating brain disease, which is like Alzheimer's and Parkinson's. Williams also took his own life.

Then I saw something that sent shivers down my spine. Hemingway and Williams shared the same birthday, 21st July. Despite the 52-year gap in their births, another question popped into my head. Were the stars aligned on the day they were born? Perhaps an astrologer can explain the parallels, but I believe it is significant.

I also believe, they were both made of the same artistic stardust. And during a moment of celestial magic and madness, their genius formed. And they were a gift to us. While a genius is compelling, and of great value to society, they are at times, troubled souls. And the normalness of life, aging, and illness, for some, is impossible to face.

A memorial to Hemingway is inscribed with a eulogy Hemingway wrote for a friend several decades earlier.

"Best of all he loved the fall
The leaves yellow on the cottonwoods
Leaves floating on the trout streams
And above the hills
The high blue windless skies
Now he will be a part of them forever."

I hope that Ernest Miller Hemingway is at peace. I hope he is with his family, and they are also at peace.

As I approach the end of this diary entry, I ask myself. Have Hemingway and Williams met? Did they blow out a candle on a joint birthday cake? While I cannot answer these questions, there is one thing I truly know. If they did meet, I would love to listen to their conversations.

The Archer – Raging Bull

London Diaries – Raging Bull

One of my prized possessions is an old DVD, of the film Raging Bull. It is one of my favourite films, but it's one that leaves me feeling incredibly sad. It's a hard film to watch, not because it's long, 2 hours and 9 minutes. It's the grittiness of the story, and it takes me on a journey of insecurity. I am sure, insecurity is something, none of us are comfortable with.

To appreciate the film, you have to be in the mood to watch it. The reason I say that. Is because, it is a serious piece of art. Similar to a Shakespearean tragedy. It isn't a film to be taken lightly, it requires concentration.

Martin Scorsese directs the film, and it portrays the life of Jake LaMotta – Born Jul 10, 1922 – Died Sep 19,

2017 (age 95). The lead role is played by Robert De Nero, for which he won an Oscar in 1981.

De Nero trained hard for this film, so hard, that he had three professional fights, of which he won two. De Niro trained with Jake La Motta, the man he played in the movie. LaMotta was convinced, De Niro could have fought professionally, if he had a mind to.

Raging Bull premiered in New York on 14th November 1980, and it was released in theatres on 19th December. The film received mixed reviews upon its release, and this was in part due to its violent content. Despite the varied reviews, the film was nominated for eight Academy Awards, and it won two. Best Actor and Best Editing.

After its release, Raging Bull went on to receive massive critical reputation, and is now considered Scorsese's most important or best work, his magnum opus.

It is also considered one of the greatest films ever made. In 1990, it became the first film, to be selected in its first year of eligibility for preservation in the United States National Film Registry, by the Library of Congress, as being. "Culturally, historically, or aesthetically significant."

The opening sequence is accompanied by Cavalleria Rusticana Intermezzo (1890)- by Pietro Mascagni. This is one of the most recognisable pieces of classical music. And to me, it captures LaMotta's anguish, his pain, and his wins and losses. Forty-three seconds into the opener, you see LaMotta. He bounces and sways. You see the rhythm that comes from someone, who knows, what they're doing. The movements are fluid, and there's no hesitation. This comes from confidence, and not from doubt.

LaMotta, was an American professional boxer, world middleweight champion, and stand-up comedian. He was nicknamed "The Bronx Bull" or "Raging Bull." He was a rough fighter, and he would stalk his opponents, and subject them to vicious beatings. To his fans, and those not close to him, he was the pride of his neighbourhood. But he hurts his family and friends. And this comes from doubt when living a real life. Perhaps, you can say, the boxing ring offers a world, with very little distraction. You are there to hurt someone, and they are there to hurt you. There isn't anything else to take away your focus.

The part that always fascinated me. Was, LaMotta went from one of the most vicious attacking fighters in the ring, and a sociopath, to a stand-up comic. And I wondered. "At what point in his life, did he make peace with himself." I've always believed, that to rid your mind of rage, takes time. It takes time to admit, you were wrong. And it takes time, to forgive yourself.

I imagine, that in his moments of solitude and reflection, there were many tears, and many regrets. That's why this film appeals to me so much. It was the first film to make me ask. "What happened to him? Is he alive? Is he well? Is he still as angry?" I had a whole bunch of questions because the film, made me ask them. I have watched many films, and very few leave their mark on me. Very few have made me question the human condition. But more significantly, this film made me look at myself. It made me evaluate, whether I had done the best I could.

This film has been described as, "a study of male rage which knows no bounds." But if you take away "the male" part, it is simply a study of rage. It is of paralysing jealousy, the need for revenge, and a feeling of inadequacy. And it's how these emotions take a physical form, in and out of the boxing ring.

LaMotta was so consumed by rage, after his wife Vickie, described an opponent as, "good-looking." He pounded the man's face. At the time, boxing had an unhealthy relationship with the mafia. You could say, they owned the U.S. fight scene. After LaMotta beat this opponents face to a pulp, a member of the mafia leans over to his boss and says. "He ain't pretty no more." After the fight, LaMotta stares at his wife, and she understands, both the message, and his fury. And this self-destructive and obsessive rage, sexual jealousy, and animalistic appetite destroyed his relationship with his wife and family.

Also featured in the film are Joe Pesci as Joey, LaMotta's well-intentioned brother and manager who tries to help Jake battle his inner demons, and Cathy Moriarty plays his wife.

Why is this film so great? I have given one reason, but there's also another. For me, it's because Robert De Niro became Jake LaMotta. He wasn't pretending, he embodied the person. Some films are great because of the action, a car chase, a fight scene, or romance. But I've often found that what we are witnessing, is the actor's personality. And that's not a bad thing, because films, just like a good book, gives flight to our imagination. Great stories inspire us, they take us to a place we cannot imagine. Great stories give our imagination a little push, and sometimes, a big push. And we try to be better than we are.

In my search to find out more about Jake LaMotta, I read an article in Esquire magazine. It was published in January 2013. And taken from an interview on 6ᵗʰ November 2012. I realised, that the fury which once existed in Jake LaMotta, had tamed, and now there was wisdom. Here are some of the quotes from that interview.

"Fighting is all I ever knew. I started out at seven, fighting in the street, fighting to give a few bucks to my father to help pay the rent. You fight to get what you want."

"I told the producer that I wanted to play myself in the movie. Raging Bull. The producer said, "Jake, you're not the type." Good thing there's a Robert De Niro."

"When you finally analyse the whole situation, you realize the arguments were stupid in the first place."

And my favourite.

"You're forced to learn whether you want to or not."

I am happy that in the end, Jake LaMotta found peace. And now when I watch the film, I also see hope.

Poetry and Thoughts

The following was a piece I wrote in 2010, since I was in a toxic relationship.

If you lose yourself in the self, the path forward is very lonely.

When you think of "I" and not in terms of "Us" you stand alone, and eventually, you will be alone.

When we sell ourselves, is our soul corrupted? A corrupted soul has lost its ability to love. The best it can do, is mimic love, without feeling it.

Do not mistake love and lust, they are not the same, and they never will be.

Love grows, it develops and nurtures the spirit and soul. Lust lends itself to abuse, it creates a lack of empathy, and at worst hatred. Lust destroys our humanity, and it leaves our souls in tatters.

On the back of these thoughts, I wrote the following poem. It also pays a small homage to my father, who I lost in 2013.

Love, Love is, Love does, Love lost,
Fathers Love, pure, supportive, lost,
Jealous love, impatient, destructive, lost,
Ego love, new, fades, lost.

Love comes and goes,
It should enrich the flow,
Of our lives,
Give it a place to grow.

Eventually on 4th July 2013, the relationship ended, and I wrote the following. It is American Independence Day, but for me, I also gained independence. I realised, you have to know, when it's time to let go.

4th July,
You left,

4th July,
I wept,

4th July,
Heart Break,

4th July,
I awake,

4th July,
Blame left,

4th July,
Start again.

And during this relationship, I often thought of my sister. I realised I had neglected her, and so I wrote the following poem.

Brothers and Sisters,
Play together,
Watch each other grow,
Fall out, make up.

Move away,
Lives separated,
Phone me?
Just busy, sorry.

I wish we could play,

We will,
I will see you soon,
Brothers and Sisters, I love you.

I wrote this following piece, as I watched my two sons growing up. I realised, this is something, we all face.

I am young,
I want to be old,
I am old,
I want to be young.

Live now,
Enjoy now,
Yesterday's gone,
Tomorrow?

From 2015 – Thoughts as I walked through London Bridge Station. I wrote this when I got to my desk at work. While the thoughts were still fresh.

I walk through the train station. I observe people jostle and push on their way to work.

They are all in a hurry. Some look annoyed, while others look confused. Perhaps confused at how they came to be here. From slumber and sleep, to this pace.

A big question crossed my mind. "How many of these people are really happy?" I'm probably not the only person to ask that question, and I won't be the last.

The question relates to their job, or what they're about to do. Are they happy with that? Does an accountant dream of another career? Perhaps, something with no numbers. Do the numbers on his spreadsheet bore him?

What does the Polish lady who works in the coffee kiosk, think of her life? Is it what she imagined as a young girl in Poland? She smiles as she hands over my Latte. I smile and I thank her. I wonder, 'should I have asked, what part of Poland are you from?' Would she think, it was weird. You have to be careful, there's a fine line between kindness, and coming across as weird.

I am abruptly stirred from my thoughts when my ticket doesn't open the barrier. People are backing up against me, the man behind me catches the heel of my shoe, and he tuts.

Thoughts of kindness disappear, as I feel a sting on my heel. People are running even later because of my dodgy ticket. Did I cause that because of my daydream, because I wasn't paying attention to the here and now? Were my thoughts of kindness as dodgy as my ticket.

After the third attempt, I get through the barriers. Head down I aim for the exit. I don't look back. I don't want to be tutted at again.

Leaving the station, I am again calm. At the traffic lights, thoughts of kindness return. I look ahead, and I smile at an old man across the road. He smiles and acknowledges me.

Thoughts ebb and flow. We must convert them to action. We must convert thoughts of kindness, to acts of kindness.

Article for Sainsburys

This is a piece I wrote for Sainsburys, while I worked there as a Business Analyst.

I presented this to their managers, who were looking to address the lack of diversity in the management team.

It explains a bit about me, but it also gives my opinion of how we consider applicants.

The Past

I grew up in Southeast London, this was during the Mid 70's. My family home was 3 miles from the bus stop where Stephen Lawrence was killed. I often used that bus stop. The people and the area were tough, and so I and others faced racism and abuse. It was an accepted way of life. As hard as it is to believe, I was attacked, because of my colour. Yes, I grew up in London, and not in apartheid governed South Africa.

Early on I learned another hard lesson. It was during a job interview. The interviewer said, "you did well in the interview, but I'm not sure how you got through the vetting process." I looked around and realised that all eyes were on me, there wasn't a single person of colour in that office. I realised that this place did not employ Black or Asian people.

But I truly believe, if you always look back on your life, without learning from it, you can never really look forward. Your thoughts cannot go in two different directions. You either go forward, or you go back.

The Present
Where we are today as a society, feels amazing, based on where I've come from. For me it feels like, we are trying to create a thriving city, on the barren landscape of Mars. From brutal racism to an inclusive world, makes me feel hopeful for my two mixed raced sons.'

I think of organisations dedicating resources to celebrate Black History Month, Diwali, Eid, Yom Kippur, and other diverse celebrations, and in my mind's eye, I see the emergence of an amazing and colourful city on Mars. The barren landscape starts to fade, and in its place, is a thriving and diverse metropolis.

Getting Better at Understanding
There is one skill managers need to improve. It is, "understand the answer."

Asians, African's, Europeans, and most people whose first language isn't English, sometimes find it difficult to express themselves.

Managers, please try to understand what they are saying. These colleagues often work hard to translate their answers before the words leave their mouths. Their brains are working on several elements, and at the same time, trying to figure out your question. They are not slow. They are intelligent.

Take a bit more time with these candidates. Take a bit more care. Listen hard to what they are saying. You may find, they have all the skills you want, and perhaps, more than you expected.

This need to understand is even more important in situations, such as disciplinaries. In these cases, consider having a translator present. This could save the organisation problems such as unfair dismissal cases.

Finally
I'll end this with a quote from Tony Robinson, "Every problem is a gift. Without them we wouldn't grow." I would add to that. Don't just see the problems, see the possibilities.

In Summary

All of us have hundreds of thoughts on a daily basis. Some good, and some, not so good. But every once in a while, we have a thought that is extraordinary, and we need to harness those.

In the moments I relax, I read, not only books, but articles on the internet. Some time ago, I read this on the following website, metaphysics-for-life.com.

"Thoughts become things when they are given substance with feelings in the Mind.

Thoughts are the DNA of the Universe. They contain the information that gives form to our physical life experience. Without feeling or substance, we would not be able to perceive the thoughtforms in our Mind.

The feelings we use to give substance to the thoughts in our Mind come from one of two sources: fear or love.

Thoughts that are given substance with fear-based feelings such as anger, frustration, or anxiety, will become things (physical life experience) that we experience as "negative" or "bad".

Thoughts given substance with Love based feelings such as gratitude, peace, happiness, and wellbeing, will become things we experience as "positive" and "good".

But there is a simpler way to understand this, and these are Gandhi's words.

Your beliefs become your thoughts,
Your thoughts become your words,
Your words become your actions,
Your actions become your habits,
Your habits become your values,
Your values become your destiny.

In writing, and in capturing my thoughts, I create something tangible. I take the idea from my mind, and I commit it to paper, or a laptop. I give my thoughts life. From these I can navigate the areas of my life I want to change, and the things that make me happy.

For me, it is a form of therapy, and I find it helps me. I believe It can work for others. If they are willing to listen to their thoughts.

But more than writing, this discipline, has allowed me to consider the past, learn from it, and hopefully make the right choices in the future.

Good luck with every single thing you do. But remember, have fun. And remember, everything starts as a blank page, it's up to us to tell the story.

Thanks

A special thanks to Kerry Coope who told me about Unsplashed.com and Pixabay.com, without which the images I've included wouldn't be possible.

Thanks to my two son's Dan and Ben, who have always supported me. And with Ben doing his A levels, I was able to read a lot of his work, and learn from it.

Thanks to Masud Uzzaman founder of The Archer magazine, and Thomas Helm, founder of Mercurius Magazine.

Thanks to the internet, without which, each article would take a very long time.

Printed in Great Britain
by Amazon

82837017R00061